Co

Co

Bruce Andrews

in collaboration with

Barbara Cole

Jesse Freeman

Jessica Grim

Yedda Morrison

Kim Rosenfield

ROOF BOOKS

NEW YORK

ISBN: 1-931824-19-3
Library of Congress Catalog Card Number: 2006923924

Thanks to Dave Brinks (YAWP in New Orleans) and Gordon Hadfield,
Sasha Steensen, Kyle Schlesinger (KIOSK in Buffalo) for publishing parts
of these collaborative texts.

Roof Books are distributed by
Small Press Distribution
1341 Seventh Avenue
Berkeley, CA. 94710-1403
Phone orders: 800-869-7553
www.spdbooks.org

This book was made possible, in part, with public funds from the
New York State Council on the Arts, a state agency.

NYSCA

Roof Books
are published by
Segue Foundation
300 Bowery
New York, NY 10012
segue.org

Contents

Bruce Andrews & Kim Rosenfield

Shootier Word

shootier prim

humanitarian rehabilitation of widows

singsong reststop

stiffing the world

Gifted bulldozing shrimp

food from our Earth

cortex chump

Cambodia

astrologizing

the clinical treatment of obesity

cling-like

noted wives and mothers

pent-up
ambient

statesmen

ease teeth up

just-for-the-hell-of-it sniper slayings

bereaving fantasy

no longer publishing a folded, color-coded guide

intenser atomics

likeliest to be bumped off

pwassions

the have and the have-nots of Italian soccer

side-effect occasionals

psycho-cybernetics

unfolds sugars
favorites

offers gasoline to would-be suicides

ruder than
adjourning

why do you mentally cringe & crawl?

a caustic artistry

come to Karachi

a matte squid

do-it-yourself tranquilizers

unsuedable
gentry

all the buzz in Venice

the mighty humid

want to change the world

pinocchio
SWAT
consequeer

Benetton Group

taste the vast

success mechanism

proof is loathsome

likened to Yoko Ono

generosity pirouette

relabel Estrogen

preferential roses

with an AK-47 pressed to my head

proverbs skiing

screen priests carefully

allure by the batch

the difference is, I came back

protocol-free

It's our way or the highway

Triage makes gadflies

how to give yourself an emotional facelift

puffoff

Just breathe heavy 3 times
and I'll be thrilled for life

desire,
commodity
pulley

but every reporter has got
to start somewhere

Do we profund?

I love that show so much
I am going to kill myself
if you don't come on next season

needle
mistake
signifier

Do not go into markets, movie theaters, parks, or crowds

one pregnant
bachelor

"sweetest guy in the world"

lather
devious

Delicious Diane in Dayton

turns
interdependence
into
sensitivity
training

when a story's good

cocoon
pleads

Tantra

don't be hasty
in your wantonness

equivalent to questioning the Pope

failing to reason
with
alabaster

and a humanitarian organization

curio
grooves

A DOWN BUT FAR FROM DEAD GRANNY

a speculative
chocolate

and key player
in the development of its atomic
bomb

who is all
reheated?

I would like to be a man
like you because you look
so masculine and popular with
the girls (with that hairy chest)

try
fermenting

a flour mill in Afghanistan

the
downtempoed

it is Christians who are the
elder brother

programmatic
delicacy

parsed without impact

smashy
made it

is Baroque better than Minimal?

paradoxes hate us

A gentleman of the highest order

money breeze
any faster

Caravan of Mercy

Never-land

perform surgery on your own thinking

underslung
be prepared

"You Fool" one of them hissed. "Y'all get us all killed."

in all its
tainted gore

ejaculate at the moment of death

buh vroom

old-fashioned
stupid
materiality

the human use of human beings

ambient
pirates

I hope this letter finds you
soaring the heights of happiness

infamous oleo

"my special son"

not to know
its own
safeguards

the benefit of speaking
good English

Labial precautionary

Your original flight schedule was:

god bless
mothball

My wife has an M.A.

grievance-purloined

secreted in his wallet

casa
curare

dumpling

the
anti-dossier

jihadi bones

uploading
every risk

the carne
asada
dispersion

we ordered cold coffee and club
sandwiches and had great chitchat

a mauve
indiscretion

"no rascality"

extinct
without hope
Yahoo is not a human being

condemn the

recuperaters

Keep our countrymen
in better conditions

gushy
tight-fitted

kidnapperguy@hotmail.com

snatched up out of
the
pseudo-indicative

the response was a
studied silence

sized
gusto
creationist
bonzai

We are inside seas, oceans, hills,
grave yards

genre
wilts

everyone in town would know

grep the
sensorial

make-up
shake-up

severity
whiskers

the answer was a "click".

glitchy
guitars

shift the patient
to the doctor

if sparks
melt

Dad has expired

spirit
in tint form
The person wielding it
seemed expert

humid &
angry

signed a book deal
+ had her baby

eco-vavoom

a shallow grave in the
garden of a nursery

madder
iris

"you got a problem with me?"

straight up Rodeo
uncut jello

bottled frapuccino

upsetted
festivals

the mining boards
automatically deploy

upgraded these
internals

take an imprint of
your lines and watch
them fade over time

keep u p your
distractions

so many taboos
so little time

viscous
as all
get out

Luck of the Irish

the graveyard of
pizzazz

a slew of revenue streams

a desperate
winterizing

failure as an education

rabbit

impossible
speculative report

any old sauce

You're going to die poor
and completely alone

favorited cabana

what's "airplane food?"

screwiest
poodle recipe

so fun away
with extra
cheese

"Sing it, Dinah"

psychic
donuts

loved only by his nanny

architecting
mercy
which surveils

Dear...Everybody!

clowns
with a brain

an honest Injun

impapped
problematicize

Those who serve you
like you

putty secular perks

the cost of loving can get
fairly steep

not the brightest
bulb in its
class

to protect the innocent

cash oh foals

it's cold and forsaken here

never enough
floating around

aren't ordinary troubles enough?

prostheses
& the
paleoughy

human sculpting

inhaltertoppably

Set! Ready! Go!

save the
undervague

Let me welcome you
warm

to modify

any misdirection

I always bag my game

"Just interrupt
the feed"—
    Black Mask
    (Hong Kong; 1997)

Collectionists like us

let the
gist begin

what beats inside her?

how big
our banditry

(with that hairy chest)

LURE
to
UNBETRAY

No rest for the
computer-generated

choke twin
mask
aphex
magic fist

it's 100 hours good

impeach
to fascinate

I'm a ripe old bird

need big escape

Not good for you health

pre-party
breeders

Feeling Sassy in Saskatoon

The former leader of a
recently disbanded commando unit
suspects that her former colleagues are
using their military talents
against drug lords in a
bloody power struggle

Baby Lady

a spaz in
TUMULT

Lifty Dren

austerity breeds
Charlemagne

20 to 1 on the David
Cassidy market

let me
swarm know

Cookie Folk

off the
iambic
cuff

Commercial product profiterole

a poached swoon
with
visiting
rights

I can always feed you and
give you liquid refreshment

o o p s

zurich vault

the butter left such a
smear on my hotpants

Citoxe

tiurf
repap
knird
eugav
ropav

Baby Marines
Violent and Cute

an alien splash

my husband will set up the goodies

half-messy

Touch your comfort

with amp
Here's There

prison the
fly

the eternal waves of
my unleashed juices

decoy
welcoming committee

Big lovable dogs. Have the cutest
Faces.

hurt
trouser
safeguards

my tropic zone number
assert the flush

headnotes

tandem
chocolate

No one minds going through
the bush to get to the circus

relax the ravage
La bataille

I can stress enough

Price: 3 adult(s) at $672.00
per ticket

clue- calming
makeup

a broad sweeping view
of the whole domain
of experiencing

half-closed

the less
I know

We always feel sorrow
when a star commits suicide, many do.

mofundi

mascara
helps police

Did the bearskin tickle?

anoint
the poosh

foster the quality of
immediacy and livingness

all stadiums
of hair

I'm a tibia freak

oscilloscope

snip a little locket
from down below

to quiz the juice

You're a lulu

dub-like

That [child] part of me is <u>so</u> hurt

formica- thighed

1/2 way between her pacifier and her
satisfier

tonight combat

mongrel
fool's gold

Well, now I can be a therapist

mercy
would have
thought

I know about a patient's personality from her vagina

autocrit at
the dilapidation
trials

You are no more like an Indian than I
am like Aunt Jemima

an essay unto
its download

Oh, yes. Let it cry.

desperately
mangling
Oh heavens to Sells Floto Circus!

overcautioned

springboard

I give a lot.

mana hula

Discussion of Excerpt H

the smell of
a trip hazard

"Did Burt Reynolds
call while I was out?"

oetic
eory

You do not argue. You just
move your foot off the person's toes

still kidding?

braggadocio
coolant

that mustache is a real
womb broom

loungier
cow
cartels

We will protect her

afterdinner perfume

Owning One's Evil

delirium
treehousefrau

send me some candy and
some jules

an atlas of all
our frostiness

with all it jams, drudgery,
and broken dreams

a cursive
black mask

I wish I could
sit on his lap

watermarked
glorying

This Helen Gurly Brown is a sickie

do I satisfact
juice the tap

organismic rightness

it's always the
quiet gestures
that get the
most done

she's despaired, despaired (exhales loudly). (Silence).

downsizing your
straps

piano at the age of 3 1/2, dance at 4,
singing age 6

lungeheads

Well, sit up then

sidelighting
at the trough

You could stride as a
GIANT ACROSS THE LAND

goobered out of
advantage

sexually yours

swizzle the gist

male meat

foam up to
greet ya

a pinkie finger-sticker-
outer

think outside skull

Most of life takes place
with other people

swell regs

Love & Tickles

to panic
without elderly

I'll be thrilled for life

righteously
desegged

what thought is, and what it is not

thimble
atmospherics

she thinks you are everything

foamy
epaulets

fashion for all

the gospel
of contrariness

You sweet body honey
send me some nice candy
or nice trinket

fabric on fiber

a padded room I need

at worst
prowl
courageous

I wouldn't mind being your son
even if you were poor. I'm sincere.

a smearing
genetics

I have friends in
the upper class

This Pilot G-2 07
pen
creates a
specific
waywardness

Note that I got it wrong

cotton
thrust

elite type

Let's
scrunch!

Childhood lacks fill themselves in

Flagrant
murk

The Superego is not moral

fabuloss
nuancities

A luster

plug-in
carboys

Who could only love
in fire

you're one category away
from smelling
bad

screaming ladies wanting to see
you nude

excuses
conquest

that's exactly what you
should be wearing

you fit
our scorch

Let's go and throw both of us
in the middle of the lake

metallurgically
careful

with frizzed bleach hair

peppery
solicits

On a scale of 1 to 10 crazy,
it's 11

didn't
breeze up

starfucker

a less
superficial
gigolo

"a truly unique harlot"

you're such
an astoriac

dritta via

reliquary
patience

I was terrified of God

anhedonist

Childhood bores the hell out of me

rave
coven
schmaltz

Iceland

inevitannunciation

take your feet into your
own hands

pushplay
aerosmithsonian

The Koran is action-packed

Your hunch
or mine

plectrum

squabble for lineage

"I should come with my
own midwife"

smudgier tarragon
tarryingly

Heights of poetic inspiration
or wisdom

hoopa retro

Tinkerhell

benzedrine
inductee-squares

between the sexes

quality
casual

clearly smitten nation

seducer lizzy

We give U 1 more day

advertise
sentiment

50 cats get personal

preacher
habit
fess-flow

the nymph turns the tables
on her attacker

insouciant
muzzling

drug-gobbling preppies

misery miniseries

the fortune came from chickenwire

fun hair,
fun prices

am I
what difference?

your chosen semen provider

multi-link
ardency

human tissue harvested
from cadavers

an
unconfabulated
tease

bioengineered sheets of
collagen harvested from a
child's foreskin

perfectibly
conflagged

silicone microdroplets

squirt
polka

what they can
tell about you in bed

juliusity

squeeze-me-tube

contagion
spiral adept

love, love, love yourself first

cheez-it
cancer
why not bet on yourself/

plump
miniseries

sexual side effects

merchandising
slugfest

Biodefensine

scrimp & scorch

even animals like to have an affair
at least once in their lives

jokier
expo

I love bassett hounds as I'm sure you do now

& in every juice

what you see is what you get

a hoopla
from the streets

If J. Paul Getty is giving something
away, how can I refuse?

nitro waft

I hope the rest of you is as
wide open as your eyes

great optimism
bad credit
I don't know what kind of a
Jew he was

pre-blond
ardency

seeker for dialogue
he was

increasing
opium

a human being in a
desperate situation

Your 80 cents a day

held responsible for events
over which you have no control

the queen
brothers

reactionary frothings

fresh
free to
learn

Sudanese dissidents
with their own axes to grind

logo museum

geo-strategic
weakness smells

jazz disarm

walking sunshine of truth

rivets
sapiens

the world lost a good one

better not be

sad, sad, sad

one more
rock farm

Have a quiet day

savoir fur
bucket of ice

ANCHORED IN ANCHORAGE

undoctoring
apology

prairie star quilt

please
quasi
spin

the crime of extortion is
libel per se

purposefully
getting a life

my brief scene involved my
walking a dog, a moment
crucial to the plot

folk rot
vacation

we'd love to have him over
for a gargle

underpuff
overpuff

"outspoken Communist affiliations"

mobile skittish

to "dignify a hurt"

culmino-lumpy

merger-office-cleaning

waltz vibe

Louis Vuitton

kiwi brill

leather goods

inside
flourish

women who screw
rockstars

idle fleeting

up downloading?

all-inclusive
carnival

local superstate

particularizing
by whim

(the decision to offer
his only son)

beat filters

a people without a land

regalia
nerves squandering

catch it at the edge
of a remark

I always sleep
on the ammunition

Mayday, losing control

nomadic
aristoclits

women's city transit

hypertriusm

all for pleasure, for joy

topography
groove

French love is a
mental game

sun-go

hypermotel

masculine, dominating,
a lion on a rock

chimp,
the otherlife

my little universe,
my mini-compund,
my own idea of heaven

shirk
some light

an orgasm a day

huge fidelity
credit
approval

I couldn't find the love

absolvent
perfectionisms

Synagogue of the Performing Arts

take control acoustics
asserted nicities

the principal of sell
as well as buy

if hemoglobin
turns to
crime

take the invigoration
home today

Bruce Andrews & Jessica Grim

Typologies

"ritual dwelling" on spec   rasta of
        scans
                smash bust-ups on how they move

                                post-defrazzled whisper
                polypalpable borderline variety
house w/out rooms lexicon w/out words
splint organic   unasleep mimic   rollercoaster
                give up
rubber cement
the lexical null icy intricate
                perfecto-infested
amiable 'abupt' all over "the dryness of the system of notation"
see-through science scrubs up   hipper than burial but... viral
ideogrammatical spelling bee
motif too entire
                        spiny & walled up
        Nonchalance   Plyable

                                        anameone
            collarbone-impacted
pollen birthing   flip betrayal   flunky   layers over layers
concentric hoax   boths & boths
                    the danger to its wager
megablock forehead switching
windows let gloom revere the pinwheel

repetitive & still warm   unit slipper

or what did you?

so many joints

"the suspended glass curtain under the skyframe..."   — my ass

accosting tains   stack me

trusses awry   view from the gap

spreader arms   to win

ytpoyogo fo teh heuos

connecting raw speedo-slick

pink plateheads "decomposing the hidden programmatic logic of the event"

degradation repetition   smackfriended

a transponder   unit gene

tap into object status oftener

trust's ambition

maze moves inward

shipshape

paper frame   buzzing starts

the padding bequest   ideo-faze   stuttery

realist threaten to serum

quiver of a dosage streak on the hip

balletic suck into

urban morphology garnish

percolator   whose torch to become

harness to trouble

you thought they cared that was your mistake

redemptive furniture periodics

deletes quotes

legit ignore width   utile

slotting around crowds empower

how an inversion vibrates

after rebate

        home alone   micro-ayatollah

bending strophe worship meanders to thaw

    self-decoder ring standing hunked up

                kick semaphore

        squigglier & unrecognizable

revival shtick as bests as you can

     arches tensed misstep restorative previous

     strap on emergency   hadn't somebody

warship militant trout   phonetically

nothing a good sentence won't cure   volumetric

geographically normalled vex

take back the ignite

        Mercator projection con art

garden variety terror   crisper duty

test   turned-up a passive triangulation

    ply the solos

eponymgo too high   'to do'

vestibule visible

   pragmatic   lucid cuts

smuggle a vestment

intimidating spurious speed

incorrigible word pronounced —

   darling fiber

   clapboard bee-line blitzed

flippant vocabulary of the stars' anywhere

      fortunately maelstrom

     meliorism

prestretch tense partial parallax

package house albatross up to enhance

subnarrative overhang you

mean removes jolt meaning right?
lend me your them
    surge protection prolonged
    name your child 'Detective'
lied to   escapism   time probe
undyingly flesh frozen   impractical modeling
Grunge
    modality design furry body
stuck up plush
    adverb clause doom
staff out the
glottal frappe
    cultivar   pilfer pillars   map
catnip dot to dot detailing
           clique all about suitable for framing
aerial   skill nova
site bliss, pliable wick   minim shock
    the familial north encore petals
    germination ovation
  generic worsted in air bump in the night
    put wings on
riff as multiply connect — you think?
    speech inhibitor don't
    think I didn't see that
go more popped over flagrant
do "buildings which might explore falls from grace, itineracy"
almost free today
    cartographers for social equality:
my dumb garden trumps your dumb garden anytime
surveillant rosette
donation defensive rebus gitgo
fingertip disquiet   an   it was but I'm not

adornment   shamelex
          job cornice razz offsets fingerless
          tinge varying delta
surveillant darkness
          hokey signatories
          grab   serenity machine   toss-off
did they get away with it?
edifying chooses not to   bonsai accordion-style
repeal
                    swizzle tense
          kit does you
earthly smear
                    to make heat plural
renege
          a verb with a mission
          scaled for jumper
at a pt of divergence smacked upon
poppy slants
where the cliché [urban sprawl] meets the outer neck
          lungful shoosh awhile   — crap!
                    how how how how how
stet unbearable prong parabolic
a preposition an integer a trigger
narcotic noun revokes   spandexical
verb reduction hygiene seismic
          good luck out of rouge
                    phylum of get the
abject wordlessness alpha undercover
impertinent & impermanent
cardiogram
          incendiary quickstep
rate at which betweens

embers

unglue   next week of locales

       deck 'em

in the exceptional language scrabble of the _____

all freedom shaggy

lips as corridor: Move Away From The Dictionary

getting your head out of the mirror

& perfume swirl

dissolve one afternoon

spatial sequences independent of, longingly

curtailed by, quicksilverishly ravishing

the meanings they evoke

       swain or pinpointed total makeover

lope along luscious inbetweens

       Ready Belief:

"conceptually, we see the project as a succession of boxes inside a box"

       boobytrap airing   skin

the deceptions of English grammar   nerves on call wettened

       hereditary moebius   no kick   pretend to vary

frighten funhouse jiggers

       quiz fervent elastic   toss-off undoing as fire

(structure form content)

       mirrors

(structure form content)

       lose the cyst   invasive shine

       as angular as bonbons

task "conceived as a series of strips placed in between a canal..."

       revenge roaring backwards

    shimmy war

       causality as gender

       those twists preside

all splay   creature features
                                a flurry of unders
"space and events become interchangeable" flamboyance
argue the blanks flunking permits
air impugn
          tart   shut up about
                                whimsical flange the wiring
"the oblique floor further challenges all perceptions of spatial stability"
                                payback
as if
or how easy —
reparations — architecture of [   ] [   ]
let's dart   (language) events

cellular intimacy for the "Sine-mover"
                    guerra / guerre
                                that creepy
grammar's interior motive
emotes   calibration versa

junket of the nouns   heat arbitrary in the crisper

slap up verb ramp   insulin
exception to the rulers

"containing no element that is functionally equivalent to the whole structure."

phrasal gumbo disappears

"A basic English sentence... is always exocentric."
          shucks quick question vamp
raffish   term point
term arc term anchor

                    stickiness   fluctuation
halve
                                        surrounds do you
                    stalactite or stalagmite feeling
vista vamp   bridge-building
                            feats of grammar
          fiancé grid   slaps at you
squeamish heights, layered
multisyllabics
units of dirt   flittings off-screen
                    place — as in placemat
cards, blocks
                    surface nook
          all the against exception to the whole
          diagonalizing for pleasure
                    tag   amend the local
as in the lexicon
a lackey on advantage
a lack of least favorite   I'm upshaft needle ahoy
                    phony
                    stature
"most language is arbitrary... however systematic its grammar"
                    cryogenic flood of
tears   smut
"the desire to have a working knowledge of the structure of one's own language."

                    [AND THEREFORE SOCIETY]
per verse   or perverse
lacquering genre screwjob
                    slab into BIG SKY
                    vocoder velocity   — lived in numbers
"blocks: quantitative functions

sky frame: qualitative functions"

getting a little desperate
        latency *conquista*
"... travelators, escalators, elevators, ramps, stairs, catwalks"
          tradecraft suddenly swamp adorable spatial guest
"... an endlessly repetitive and neutralized grid"
            believes the bang
suitcase moraine
      without servo
    calamity-ish
            UP A[F]GAINST serious sweet
            kingdom repieced

"...the recursive power of a grammar... [overages loosened allure post-abstinence] is its ability to generate an infinity of sentences."

snack trying both mothball the slander
           ambition punk dismay

"... by extending a single piece of architecture over the entire world they could 'put cosmic order on earth'"

de-slang fenestration   job as a cave   — to make slicing cosmic
typology of the house
        greenhouse fooling smear goo extenders
step into the quizshow thaws
lexeme web snatch frontier   helter-skelter
      plif xaohy soahc
    TOWARDS
a lexicological term IS self-study
        space is an ambush

interactively decked out

                           — do we fret over it?

a past we are still experiencing
             [AND THEREFORE SOCIETY]

autonomous architecture generator

postdrug bargain-hunting when on

cognate object oompah
       insipider

classic sentence orders leaning is done
       you're not
divorced 'over your heads'
                       enough interiorized judging
from   meaning   gallows less clubbable

cleptolingua & learn how

beach glass protract mousse deficit

spot-on, Bob
            losers' ballrooms

random reigns
totally
random resigns

        clingy docket   special solvent
gradience totems lock in the cuts as if

arbor as in

suggest delusion on a cross

intonement   lipids: crime pays
against against
on to its gumption
          articles upriver on
      to rebuild the tallest statutory disappearance
earthly

                            Thy
      scourge   drum up insistences
          all achey with nostalgia for
deflotation
retaliation
azul anil   procure hope claw the usual
blood to the chaser
      tertiary twinge of
labial consonant
      turned just so the façade
air blotted pierces
ill-framed if-clause
         solicitation memory
         eyeballs' enmity
exothermic wig-out empty as ripe
adjectives on meds shapely
                colloquially fighting kingness
      tangent other
not-not
      worldly skin of
bogus lamé socially spurious
      the bldg a kind of

cape keen bed   typifies   lame   from the on
      heart comes unattached   button climax
         crushed mouth mud-filled neutrality typecast
     daredevil sleeping on it
blue-blonde: my doorway from hell
predicate fluctuate   flight nodding flip out of this
      well turn my tin head 'round
           gentle thug
illicite chrome cruise you?
          palpable tropology on ease
flask trauma
 And not another line
The potential mode of irrealis
     Expletive *it*
       parabola crystal switch

terminally adverbial   flora reverb
exterior structure masks the
system's slots: word seepage
fast forward to escort despite the flaws
awakes nonmeditative rage
dipthong hog-wild odometer guardian
incubate gerunds for peak performance
            reassign the chops
     fling
mimic feigning remorse ad
    nauseum crisp tone down
ethos   tempo of planetary
  nomenclature
    orbitally challenged
positionality vis a vis retro
to meaning   straight

lines   display patriotism's bunting
        a spartacus of verbs
flank   hinge   barometer
pestilence   moody craw
genetically modified   vermin sprig
    plunge keel where goes I
seeming still
  up it
caverns by the sea housed
curious rigor mops
    stet sound
        anyone?

Bruce Andrews & Jesse Freeman

Or Possible Elsewhere

1.

yrreM
samtsirhC
[touchdown Jesus] full-scale layout
halo drop-off
l'etourderie un oubli
stars EDGZ & flats bled to bone
Quit messin' around!
Quit messin' around!
cut pattern interior dome
don't reveille cat sleep
le Fais-Do-Do
Angelino filé transglitter
Embroidery Whitsunday
God is a drunken lout
by God, zydeco closely guards moss-hung courtyard
red ice cream scoop
sloe gin barges fizz saint francisville
slow drift downrivr
croissant marzipan bayou cadillac
crab claws apricot Greek Revival
metal parasol
'tit fer frag gateless padded axle
time is present always and is hard to erase

le grand dérangement
unGodly balcony overlooks vanishing
point absolution? Forget it
wishful wistful lava in driver seat
"What does that mean?"
"It doesn't mean anything."
uncountrying the X-Possibles
far sud: El Archangel Barachiel 1604
she is dead in the water
panic's timpani & strychnine
quake past aspens far north...
non-fairy tale ending variant
ANABASIS — Broken Egg Café
Atomic Adam bibliophilic altered states
Meringue lemon pie
Twice in blue moon sudden death
ad hock novena bckwrdness
found stuck tween book pags
tchoupitoulas allons danser
tilt-a-world more mulish
JUXTA   Open 24 Hrs
owe the pastels
WORTHY IS THE LAMB
WHY IS THE LAMB
Gras zip puff onto lazuli
"zzfiz ecc fizz cch fzz
fffiz ecc hizz cch ris"
click it, commute this sentence
Congressional Record proofreader
liqur hurrican papier mushy
Day 3. New Orleans. Hello Elysabeth
 font us up, snapshot snaps shut

proscenium double-cross

blintz fleece chicory edge peepers delight

tip of voodoo price of infliction

disinvertebrate line tied up chintz

young pigeon neath gravy beans H20melon loblolly

quince jelly catfish sans leek chilies chops

hack into aps opaque could talk

OAPBOXESLE

orbit stuffing atrocities of faith

Luz IOTA

walaa!

you cannot swoop south

errantry

Meringue pie

Sudden death

trump fate gris on gris

too orleans map in mix

retrace your deepsouth routes ! !

oyster po-boys git it or git it

point blank blues

mere close range

mere backaway close range

Belize breeze ukelele

le le le le uke

licorice jurisdiction dogwood soufflé

a meatless amen subtle

bruising on vapor spangles of

creasey press grisaille déjà preview

magnolia etceteras hurry up, gate

toponyms in sout Loosiana

disguise is out of the Question

bingo info redress counterfeiters' slabfest

fizz just takes no pincers
method hurricane prin' bleu fiddlesticks
title   prendre des risques inutiles
le bureau des objets trouves
Operation Archangel
alphabeaut Innocenciad agave rule
successive bunny skins' deveinage
oysters rice peach... bullseye
jiffycut psalms Vieux Carre
chipotle indigo popcorn
Oyez voodoo acade arcade bunkum
snake sugarcane French this week
crank shines etouffey choke up redecor
Camp & Magazine
'Do it now!'
strawb Galatoire panopt
sais-tu ce qui m'est arrive hier
lowride redipper bottle-rockets & beef popsicles
bully slab tetrahedron relapse blast
aha silly cloth billboards
ricochet up perfect gizmo bloodfly gypstic
coconut mounds sugarfine pilotpoint
southern gulf floats & distracts & dresses occasion
pent up pry faux zip: insight wipeout
stet bargain streamline horn-slide
Enragé
scratched away with
creatures I see are inside-out
insides everywhere
free range evil astronaut wishlist
may it meltdown r'here bbrr
Bluerunners just cream allelujish

on houses many colors
one beneath the other
geechee apostrophe, over easy
Iko Iko
for publ
Plus-mas kilos per
all showing, surfacing insides out
Chez Personne (No Man's Land)
Kamra Obskura

2.

You spoilin me
IN ACTION
extreme keen in
resizzle counterfeint
bubbles & cake
writer of this letter to elysabeth UNknown
i quite like his take on the easy
I write to you from the city of great noises
the city where all who move are dancers
and so much work it takes to live!
hunch nite pas-de-uno loopy lull bolt bleu
shelter in Evangeline emergency brake
The Armbender
take pinball personally
coming your neckwoods off
paramedics' spoon chin cram lilt y lilt y lilt
tossing self divorce gala oct 5
come
!

curvilinear CHOCTAW gland lite

snakewater through penis vanilla finale —

did you loose?

for low many yrs call quits am bored need new directions

far altogether far too late in the game

mo-noun retrouted craw- waif euphrates

pentecost

valentines

tussle veer mule minute midnight minutes

telltall gimcrack quizzy collidin

when is today for you?

how many miles between us?

expectation breeds commas

"It is a lot easier

to find a victim than it is a listener." — serial killer, *The Mean Season*

hurt male DIZZY SPIT untouché

drink to tha

turns down horseflesh giddy yap nightdamp

imposter imperative modular pinholes booze

in the tightrope with appropriate burlesk

You deliberately/determinedly involved them in criminal activity

under the guise of AGRICYGNUS

PURPLE PATCH

stop gap blues

drag king ducktail iconic prorated scent

valise packed she's out

outta here cette semaine

late in the game

he's got umbrella stand

au lait bidet

what he won't got no more

Marisa

Marisa stop gap woman
 waiting inside his door
these meatsticks grenadined singsong upkeep
cette semaine
cette semaine
out out late in game
lift-off DNA innocents
aint nice water maid hush up shh shhhh demon sex
grief help shimmy icky wet
to endgame's une mitraillette la defaite
spit it out spit it out spit it out spit it out spit it out spit it out
spit it out spit it out spit it out spit it out spit it out spit it out
spit it out spit it out spit it out spit it out spit it out spit it out
spit it out spit it out spit it out spit it out spit it out spit it out
hunker over setee, pat hand on its guilt-a-thon
longest bloodywinded nightmare
obscene scean domestik
tah tah
april fools
trois menage
lose
yearn to burn, yearn too soon
he's up on hindlegs
aldface lies
PLUS QUE PARFAIT
bayou follow-up queensize mattress
@ heart he's a rover
cachet ask fo self-pat
POSSIBLE ELSEwelts
epoxy love lick leer
ghastly asshole husband of 35 nitemare yrs sending sheriff
in a week serve divorce papers he war @ war will not

grant divorcee iron fist control 65 yr ol man aint bout to release

hey baby, quoi ça dit?

open wide || strangle

open

lingerer-proof sugar creamed fuss

Your own brothers disown you

prison d'amour mam pap mammal makeup

whim patience anecdotal crap

pillow lies soaking wet

extremely ill going down steady

slide loathsom little time

upqueer carefree gotcha boyo

impov vanity à go go

and introduced them to the homosexual lifestyle

against their natures & desires

Storyville digs hooker psyche

boogygal perox' all butched talk bad

Thirty-five brutal years stand as a testimony to the fact

you harbor hate not love

mbouch edge hug to the max

thrown for loop dark glasses

mask effort to step key up

step into storybook love

swag limb curtsy blowback mono-immaculated

havoc has a home

She drags feet

Picks up evidence, lipstick, unknown bra

Wages of sin

shade no high tea, forget hammock supine

drop it or I drop U

changer de vitesse adieu

svelte git the eccentricized redlight

fanciful briomatic shiner —

what makes you so sure?

activity look upspoon replay easy sausage

corrupting the nicknames, aubergine you too

Me an example

But I tell you, I'm not degenerating

or papaphobia

Obviously, your refusal to give me what i most need and desire —

divorce — prompts this missive

"This line is tapped so I must be brief." — Morpheus, *Matrix*

again & again he kills imbibes

misbehaves on Hobie relays]sic pussycat name kingfish

keeping you from agreeing to terminate this charade/bondage

exhort swallow

Uneasy Story

better angels of our

susan's gigolo killed her 9 yrs ago

my soulmate heartache twin

both born jan 25 1940 me in L.A. susan in K.C.kansas

Carnival god convicts

him to aloneness

no limits

back at you

harbors the fear you will come gunning for me

IF I finally manage to break away from you

heart[ship]shape

sad-sack-Gide falls gets stomped on proposin

elegiac heights seven feet below sealevel

pucker down fake malign

here, now, Pentecostal whores oversee

painterly Josephine, le grand amour de Napoleon

à la funkadelice accuse

all who have witnessed our sordid saga know

you not only never have loved me, you don't even like me

you are a bitter hate-filled being incapable of

genuine loving thoughts and emotions

both now majors

precious beef of highhandedness

those who have known you over the course of your sorry life

abbreviated pinkie uterine gabfestive catcall

demitussle she'll

divvy up

go spit

go away

dismantle ensue   reach go

she

WHEREFORE Petitioner prays for a judgment of divorce from the

defendant, forever dissolving the bonds of matrimony existing between

she

de mes sentiments les meilleurs !

so when do you get this?

tip top nothing indulges the wick

sugarbreath frappe body frazzl

herein wearable T

diz spit

spit it out !

anti-yes

a normal human being who must participate in Life

who must interact with others

A woman does not sink into horrific spirals of

hopelessness and utter despair that is valued and RESPECTED

 and honored by her husband

anx de brazos

incise lips

3.

Repeat Chorus
we'll kick as close gap tween union/confederates
territorial ?
pentagonal How2 krush or prefuse
intox guilty kooked sense folksed-up
material isthmus to serve crème brulee
& Justice on half-shell
on leisured-class wall fluent graffiti + -
SCREW monksee do vieux carre ramPart
FELL SWOOP teach you a lesson
extremely ill little time
boss linger vile-orama skid along tabu
pomp & circumstance prop bootlegs
on razor-wire as well as Dante
norms gook full of reflex camera shy lullapalooza
on jet ski
bangup job
bangup job
let's go   go   avanti
jerky juridical privilege jettison rogue dramatization
"Degenerates are not always criminals, prostitutes, anarchists
& pronounced lunatics; they are often authors & artists"
frontpage snowcup
WORTH
JACK
SHIT
NO CRUSADES
KONFLUENCE and juke joints of the
askew politic schmaltzoclast highriders
help link me to b&w lit zines

godless humidity & propaganda make a dash for it

allelujah looks back to die

mythologize ooze officer braille

robber pokes head up

unsooner freedom no substitute

mad cow feedback sacred ecumenical dieu

autopsy vandalizing mash Common

know anywhere to job this?

peonage placemats — smooth as debt

apparatus fanciers greasin forty

lullabye babe andalusia aint west texas aint Valladolid

vat d hell Ibanez vincente blasco 4 horseman

of d apocalype transgress klondike fever pitch

bodycount formality doub back big piety gap

le bon ton roulet

swears dramatic effect has yet to paint

Freedom into a corner, in daze to come

Mamou's Sostan dangercase muck-up

rodeo days surrender weapons

drastic sucker jumpy dollars drive

Justice blink drunk

just dessert: bail

the Other, polyester pirate defiance

amigos !!

join our FREEDOM FIESTA

when: october 5th

time: 4 to 7 pm

hear: señor hector mendoza & his mariachi band

where: 1721 manor oak drive baton rouge

see you soon

mini-ape in between

dive bomb the king roi

the surface carnal good guys

speSHEaleetaye

globlly bckbited gumbo raja hell with zoot

canoe yolk-yellow drifts longside junk male

nearby molehills hunger

hackberry rambler gang raffish two-step jargonicity

legit strut aw greedier

NO DICE

NO DICE

Ponchartrain witnesses, Clinton witnesses

mademoiselle get back

cool avant

fuck your private opinion

"Literature is largely although not entirely

the product of maniacs"

justice worthless widowmaker switch

on the personnel gifts nothing, nada

trois menage

shoot one tw

zipgun, zexpress

more & more ask to produce personal walkabout billboards

boire briller bouillir entrer hurler

a toy court full target rake

Marigny psygeog

dowager Mademoiselle age 72 Lilly Pfeiffer

upon her east wall burnt ochre Duce Mussolini

spy fresco debt-ribbed pills 'n' Lafitte

to nomadize

madcowrampagemadcowrampage

rollback faction, containment faction

assassi- nepotism

Warlord Blues

Deliver us
Deliver Us out from under evil
antebell'
Negra Modelo rasterize yourself, trickonauts
interrupted by goon squads' Dread
Luisianne gaga state O union
One-man-militia
Son of a gun
don't mix freedom & opinion
the Hebrew talking carp —
be damnd ! meat pies' goopey bastard heir
red tousle hair nevertheless, a belch, a poignant
Maison de Amis & Chez des Amis 11 Washington Street
His bro-in-law gluttonous hear! Don Vappie & Creole Serenaders
 who knows polygamists
Warlord under this tin roof
Warlord, Lordin it over me & my sons
whitey alias shogun zulu
You subject my sons and I in abject poverty
You owe me a great deal of money
narrative buzzard — not in our name
no-man's-land rattletrap'll fail to brake
graveyard Number Questionmark
self outta
Commander's Palace runaway thong-fists
25 cent martini Social Science
let us now prop men
NOLA NOLA NOLA NOLA NOla mere pastime
FOCUS THIS
rules roles ebb or vict tearsheetoff
Bloody well Lords it over us, he does
Warlord

War

Warlord, Lord God, He Lords it to Kingdom come...

amenities none, no, not an iron balcony

highway 61 robbery

blunt lil atom Mr. Taco mogulized

ordinary children mail-order some

baboon rubs up against zydeco

washboard against stigmata's sin

& vermillion holes

last gutter shot in the sham de rigor

a wonderful beautiful mess

enemies get laid off

dollars drive neural interactive simulation

zac zhll ajill ete ntrum rum rumms tantrum

eeooO eO sac zhll ajill ete nronze tante rumba brum

hemorrhagic dazzle to surveil

blowJob Bohemian

upside down stalker —

"most of these people are not ready to be unplugged" —

Abita make a Dark? —

glad rags une recompense

thinks you deserve obliteration for your cruelty and ruination of me

TKO-avoider: Rome wasn't burned in a day

not a motherF amenity be had privy bath suite

grabby up straight parvenu re-mount

are on serious Federal and State "kook/crackpot lists"

the very definition of loner — freak —

you are friendless by choice and anti-social

pokey glam krewe blast

guilt gangsters kooknut dopeyellow bloodsplash

of course a copy goes to CITIZENS BUSINESS BANK and money
managers

you recently tried (unsuccessfully) into conning access
cruisier fanciful melange
choppers style FBI blender
spit to witness somersault impact
zodico... haricots... opt ops
solder blurt flap arc scary elevated
sazerac invent hum'n'coke
oven payout
need preferential treatment
Christmas in a glass
epaulets for brains

Bruce Andrews & Barbara Cole

Gilding the Lily

A.

attention: now firing
scratch your itch
dishy crayon auto-rigor disbuttal
stop the spinning, simplify the evasion —
do you read me? —
feign rupture
overpruned softie truth, gullibly readerly
paramedic merch lexicon multiplex nuh huh
the oomph factor
whatcha thought checks
assumptive nice touch disclosure disclaimer
typographically mushy like a waterbed, steady-cam —
are you name dropping again? —
all nutty miracles, but eraserhead is too life-like
opiated hunters & gatherers
wedded blisters — no glitter there? —
event sequence of fictional units trades places with you
a predisposition for past tense narratives
all slathered, get it while it's hot —
creepers, where'd you get those bourgeoise delusions? —
always to *have been* a fancier smear —
are you getting me? —
eat the prep, to 'do' the deficiency
this end up, little bethlehem

mauve disney minotauric disengaged insistence

to do the decoy object topoi in different decodings:

it's the eye of the buyer, it's the thrill of the sight

preoccupied when lit

may cause greasy discharge

giddyup, el destructo

desperately seeking stupid precocious prepster stump-puppets

the line starts here, confusing my pronouns

pack it up boys, spin forward &

big antlers, bunny rabbits on the back of a jackhammer

now it's just a cause of positioning

pa rump a bum bum siege under system —

beat until smooth heave upon the intrudes

bunch up rescue slap-happy jibber jabber

needforspeed goober binary

deaf and numb mini-er:

YOU ARE HERE

species-matic blur info

stir gently, topspeed is safe

tagline huffing swerve into size

supplies are delimited

vocabulary alteration

wrongful dunce into a corkscrew

a tri-state vulnerability to pry the mold forward

a seeming unlikelihood should be taken seriously

how to do things with Kurds: 'going manual'

vehemence without stress

paper peel waxy discharge

we are beginning our descent...

B.

Frighten your git-go ahead:
gild my lily
existentialism for minors
mystery crashpad bottom feeder
I mean, like, ambiguity, dude
it does a body good
gangful & sustained employment...
"Inspiration will strike when least expected"...
five finger this jet us up shut
hit me with your best shit
pupcake, costumerelations
I'm all hacked out
listening and listless, anonymous gave in
heat up versus heat down cunning content piss stop
fake it to the heart, the accusatory 'huh'
a mattress does just make curious
Ink to Heart: Daytime, sue me —
jump the gun freedom flighter, no other
diaper stops leaks better
& I don't have to go write now...
"You will get it all done"...
the hyperresponsible thing:
time for a break, self-proclaimed twist tease
T I M E T O P A N I C
putting the man back into manicured
isn't quite what I had in mind
redefining 'forthcoming'
to be exhausted to be salty
throw me a bone, rinse your power
melts in your mouth, not in your hand
rinse the vanity off

bio got to be sweltering
manhandle my panhandle quiver koan:
when did *tender* get to be a monosyllable
to specify the emotion ahead of time
put your mouth where the money is &
fumble over the connotes, the mantra of auto-reg:
bite me off a piece of that
the father, chronic disappearer's
money grows back
slated in blather & expected to like it
please bow for head sexhibitionist
for a bruisin'
eat my skirts
does it get more wrapped?
was it the phrase 'pussy juice' you found off-putting
or the basic sentiment?
is disdain getting all the good pieces?
lathered in disappointment:
what that says about you —
liking the dark parts best
hrumph guilt, overhabitat yourself
all stumped up with nowhere to
CARE LESS
giddy up my git along
doggie-style research
I'm not overcrawling —
can it fling the they?
whip until stiff, total stunt
towel off
pat never rub
jerk your baja: revelatory melancholy
communicative else can you think of

neater pills
recommended by Dr. Mom
the contrasubservient *mami* —
why am I not surprised?
distraught without a trace
putting the come back in communication
a strange hand on the neck, sad-eyed hurry
go ahead & question it —
that won't make me any less serious
sure of your slob?
folic or frolic
I'll let you take your outlandish bit of stuff away:
open your mouth wider

C.

Formalism, stop sulking —
girl, who told her she could wear that? —
lasso listens
rubberized ego armor
seize the treat of its smear cartel
whimsical why... wish your mulch
merthiolated mirth machine
polymorphous — call me poly:
she stoops, she stores
grandstanding prowess, a case of the kilt
betraying that particular brand of regret —
choosy Moms choose different Dads:
aren't you excluding misstructure? —
bride or bribe shtick connotes
I'm very proud of this vehicle

tastes filling, less great

freedom's just another word for strong arm

of the law lock jaw bugger badge

reverb, Mr. Scooter

now that's a superfuckinmarket

jack-off lantern & candy porn —

didn't I dialog up your crawlspace? —

train me up, train me down

tit for tat & me for that —

may you give up in first class

a guillotine with a continental kit

pissed off halloween costumes

harder to manhandle

who's inclined to police —

why would calling it 'the boob tube' make me

less inclined to watch? —

protest the clock

most watched harassment

a licked-up pick-up line

promises overtime, location-specific kitsch, her

feminism being of the if-she-watches-soaps-

she-deserves-to-be-subjugated variety

XXX,XXX,XXX

SOCIAL SECURITY NUMBER on your

husbandry as ghosting

curfew supplies

tourist trap tittie tassels

blood on refund, ever forcefeed? —

a supermarket at the end of your rope

the ass is finally 'safer' in mass culture

storms mostly or all socioeconomic

bottomless mobility

deregulated dum dums for the lacking
outslaved the calm before the loot
'hegemonic' v. 'dicked up' —
is you is or is you ain't
my assuaged white liberal guilt
okay vic transitional metaverb
a disloyal blues
dow jonesing a greed instructor
scam that grow
oh, go fuck your 'student loans'
granny panty ideology
my nation so disconcerting, trickle down this
terror imprecision
faculty dies a virgin
power power

Bruce Andrews & Yedda Morrison

Puppy-Skills

1.

Tinsel without spotting. Icon nicely help the hooded with lexical lupus. Who can outmarshal the facts or facilitate eye-witness. Underload episodic perishable spot check expunges lucidity [independent variable]. Transistorating tap root lashed against the least common denominator. A nice exit vested photo op some calmer diagonals dismiss. Natural selection recycling impli-care atoms.

expedigit detour
twizzlers loop axiomatic
of genetic lemon-lime ballistic
scrub thee
suspends
error bravado hook
sudsier than
white gob where the corners meet silence
ordered the
nuclei hatchet job
with blood sweat &
prone in a goody prim
wee what-
have-yous peeping out

Pilot chimps denatured lies. Spores breeding focal length blizzard infection alarmists stay untouchable in. Monochromatic pre-emp the demale periphery. Sleepers become expectancy index to the same hysterical site.

truce on chronic poetiquette
shiny & non-responsive
flat & shadowy
transgoners
with their transponders overboard!
offqueering soft twin
saliva bouquet eyeball clutch
bound with satin ribbon sensation
full of perma-vague
opiated wonder charm
get rage
polished 3 time loser
wants the goolight
a measuring worm
outed as an input
damn-
dead textbook
sidesaddle tibia
quick hinge
buick-brittle
hatch-back
half-life

Every wet of the way forager entitlement enthusiasms armored diffusion. Lime on every bite of a stale four star serving. Discoloration disclaimer — imprint the sheen bunnies, carbonize desperate imperfect fungus gridlock. Flamboyance candy is a mixed bag daddy.

Beginner's Object — mine?
polyurethral
unlabored exists?
the dossier! the dossier! ladies! the dossier!

you're beating me at my own game
inside pep imaginary
miry crack exterior
it takes one to flammable diaphragm
itches majorly general
filly fringe arounder
primarily insuccessive & guilty
a cephalic index
never a
frothier beast
hold to my enlargement
minutest access
a thimble lobotomy but
a   non the less
snap
someone else's outfit
looks better when you *use* it

2

Hatchet job quotes anthracite pre-impact exotic jungle bonsai. Blind
ceremony catharsis as bride heaves over beautox. Melt that meat for
the dainty memorialist. Proverb factory goes down in rain check.
Tadpole to the stars grew legs & wallowed there.

care prehypo
caveats of bracing
freakshow
without a net
mock the slick

dick the smock
safety in hummers?
televizzle crumbcake
double disco diaper
clairvoyance in beat structure
cemetrical & smokey blue dechlorinated sideshow
pissed in it
a flagon of speech
when needing water
ticktock amateur

Resizzle sully bang on pressure cashmere in a mangy man-grove.
Pickpocketing regress in gowns of slash & vinyl. Kneeling uppers near sighted
& gabby. Tuck rubric skin graft indigenous scrotarium offers free parking &
popcorn. Happy hour is over so have another drink.

polkadot
skirt bombs
the cash & carry
rash is right
below my bible belt
flesh à la mode
performative pie queen
no thanks
turn up your parental cooler
chicks is gonna roudy
wider than choice
the house is empty
my bloody serviette
affect lever cranked
fetal cues in cabbage patch
border this crap

Cornhusk kisses blur family bible bauble blood gun metal keepsake. Expectancy's roadkill swerves the corvette — snowcone mini-mastery. Lather on buzz vox relief valve for upwardly blast yogi. Sardonic recurring decimal orchids on the fly-by. It's a wrap around number with button down appeal — it-bops on a dolly frost.

I Speak Banana Republic
a leisurable crutch going sideways
mall rat-like
rotarianitis
bit me bad
finite as the dickens
if dickheads were bookends
taster crank grim upwish
wealth impeccable
as slasher-wear
a rump of irony
humble piercing popular encrudding
waist high in it

3

As if or though the wish mill. Knife-like passivity quake orchestrates recess regret & other absolute childhoods. Egotism rev up accretive ragdoll over obituary reject. Mutually marriageable pre-equality portion skirmishing SIDS eclampsia. Entirely tremor-dependent when dissipating heart-shaped fireworks.

Animalismo

interiorized debt
s'cravings and groan under-tallest
with a taste for over-achievers
dysfunctional codpiece
making come back as cockchafer
tongue per miniature
per get up per tip
teeth on barbie
tits on ken
longing on the house
"Fuck you" in bold caps
backup pronoun
Hey! I'm saving that
uncontrollable tissue ache
spotty lass-production
lop on dander stick

Testimony aggravates hetero advocates. Zip-up laureate — handbag
indexical yet female toxicity breath per faction. Romance, an arbitrary
licking. Seminal reactive volitional nuance vista rapidity, measures of
near miss. Precision prudence regrets the million that got away.

nervous outside
anxiety nub
bunnies on the *shhhhhh*
it manages our breath away
lantern jaw akimbo
spearmint tongue depressor
compliance snuggles up
I'm your venus
spinning preacher's samba *fatale*
shambling prank beginnings

play the roles
fake out serenade
glue-pot incantation
sudsiest schoolant implosive ambiance
dear sir

Puppy-skills in the cubicle daycare. Headkick dryclean one hour rift
breaks twin-set hegemony — a soluble weighstation enterprise. Zing
beyond the missionary position on the blips. Her radioactivity com-
plex über-clit über-alles. Yipes! My credentials!

radioactive genitalia
hot crotch is neon
chloroform nascent
narco
flesh off exit
my kissing cousin mushy & impulsed
to love without organs
pupate us, hon'
sparerib feminism
with major back-splash all but crusted
postpartum + ticking
ovular ignition
light me up
I never start
rather not leave
what *wasn't* nylon
where I found her
to begin with was
nylon then & after

4

Sensor hands make 1/2 the work. Access to declension babier
mooing for new world turkey vultures. Oatmeal leaves Empire bloat-
ed free at night. Little slaves lapelling storm to scratch & scratch land-
scape psoriasis to warn international high watermark, teleprompter-
fluent. My ticker tape waistline, our Amtrak gorilla nape on smack.

Fear the blow
spoil the child
touché goop wham then wham again
in line for work
pugilist grace a people's catheter
function ups ante
a line-up squandered
dissimilar products
dead-heading leftists
on & on
to the devilish present
impulse turbine implementarium
craven pronoun landgrabber
blurt
before we could chop that chicken
without might or nuance
's moral panic
"you want boots or flipflops" (election billboard)
privilege immunizes
net weight nuclear
boyish public goes pubic with dismissal
cherrybomb your rights
picnic rupture bumbled

Any fucking deadtime is better than no deadtime at all. Fingerprints belong to history's fusillade. Postlarval inheritance hop on option props this leadership's discursively chunky sinking rutish hovercraft. Oval as in assassin correlation as in conquest. No, *you* are the clear & present danger. No, *you* are.

utterance becomes cotton
"cotton kills in the back country"
who tears whose heart out
revisionist history underspecified agents
in dispute over legalized hygienes
rest at sub (sob?)
eat at sub
wash at sub
fuck at sub
work at sub
sub at sub
econo-sh t
save where you can-can
teflon sentence structure
has 'em bushwhacked
a prayerful hack
and he's back in business
didn't...   LIFE ALERT...
the action package
anti-social cheat sheet
gave me your numbers

Global harming doesn't exist?! "Away away away Fidel y Che." Citizen detainee dressed as one ice cream vendor to harangue charity feudalism. To rehabilitate the crowd: "Everybody hurts sometimes" [REM LIVE 8]. The warping of affect due to ideological requirements of wage labor in wading hose. Sili*coneheads*, all rise!

zapata junior in supersized Guevara
denaped our empire waistline
gouging: skin or price?
what's diff?
babies without helmets
you wouldn't would you?
event stuff smudged
cash or carry
biomechanical flipper
beats a pretty picture
pitchfork your profit
Heh is for has-beens
reviva police
got you lookin perky
keypad larynx
say it again Sam
galvanize the self-actualizing
weeds (or weed out) mayhem

5

Tonguists self-surrender spinal crankberry. Micro digit grace period or
collective juvenilia — oopsy pre-op gargantuan space needle.
Intelligence crumbles — the nonviolent forcep disarticulate cake walk
for gladiators.

anonymity speaks up
you got words for that?

with a tongue that big
let's worm the sky
Or: am I evangelical enough?
throat delete misadvise pamper
undo undelete
laugh to skirt
our complete lack of landing craft
osmosis on the git go
it's rough & ready
finite enough for you?
for the exit buzz generation

Kill locale. Yogic jitney razor castes fuel fresh fruit colonic. Newsy perk on mass ghost writer, systemically squalid life buoy mannerism on provost. *STOLEN FROM THE WHITE HOUSE* — rare earth metals & organs. Automatic facework for beaver tailed boomers.

try this frequency cruncher
prefab torso patent
rubber arrears
artel casino
retroexpo dispenser, bio-hesitant
because we'd been there
simulatedly awkward
seedless, boneless, bingeless
ginning goner up
road winds straight ahead
ah ah multiples
how they tic
true tales of translucence
won hands down

Manifest horror stuck systemic igniting poppy doubles disaster. An impossible morale motto caretops unspool. Rendezvous, perforate your space. Inject isotope for metamorphosis factor that imperial light may enhance your periphery. Hopped & hoped the isms in charge. Ideology flicker, for instance — dizzy, elated, allegorists of the aberrant pixel.

jigsaw workability sugars
4 X 4
pinch bunk
tender flagstone
lexi at last
rules get anti-crap
anus gets the tight squeeze
rouge nightlit & lived-in
doll ringlets out into the metropolis
griefer than thou
oh balance of powders
singe what local
post larval moodring
sawing septums
touché oval
let me touch yours

ROOF BOOKS

Andrews, Bruce. **Ex Why Zee**. 112p. $10.95.

Andrews, Bruce. **Getting Ready To Have Been Frightened**. 116p. $7.50.

Benson, Steve. **Blue Book**. Copub. with The Figures. 250p. $12.50

Bernstein, Charles. **Controlling Interests**. 80p. $11.95.

Bernstein, Charles. **Islets/Irritations**. 112p. $9.95.

Bernstein, Charles (editor). **The Politics of Poetic Form**.
  246p. $12.95; cloth $21.95.

Brossard, Nicole. **Picture Theory**. 188p. $11.95.

Cadiot, Olivier. **Former, Future, Fugitive**. Translated by Cole Swensen. 166p. $13.95.

Champion, Miles. **Three Bell Zero**. 72p. $10.95.

Child, Abigail. **Scatter Matrix**. 79p. $9.95.

Davies, Alan. **Active 24 Hours**. 100p. $5.

Davies, Alan. **Signage**. 184p. $11.

Davies, Alan. **Rave**. 64p. $7.95.

Day, Jean. **A Young Recruit**. 58p. $6.

Di Palma, Ray. **Motion of the Cypher**. 112p. $10.95.

Di Palma, Ray. **Raik**. 100p. $9.95.

Doris, Stacy. **Kildare**. 104p. $9.95.

Dreyer, Lynne. **The White Museum**. 80p. $6.

Dworkin, Craig. **Strand**. 112p. $12.95.

Edwards, Ken. **Good Science**. 80p. $9.95.

Eigner, Larry. **Areas Lights Heights**. 182p. $12, $22 (cloth).

Gardner, Drew. **Petroleum Hat**. 96p. $12.95.

Gizzi, Michael. **Continental Harmonies**. 96p. $8.95.

Gladman, Renee. **A Picture-Feeling**. 72p. $10.95.

Goldman, Judith. **Vocoder**. 96p. $11.95.

Gottlieb, Michael. **Ninety-Six Tears**. 88p. $5.

Gottlieb, Michael. **Gorgeous Plunge**. 96p. $11.95.

Gottlieb, Michael. **Lost & Found**. 80p. $11.95.

Greenwald, Ted. **Jumping the Line**. 120p. $12.95.

Grenier, Robert. **A Day at the Beach**. 80p. $6.

Grosman, Ernesto. **The XULReader: An Anthology of Argentine Poetry
  (1981–1996)**. 167p. $14.95.

Guest, Barbara. **Dürer in the Window, Reflexions on Art**.
  Book design by Richard Tuttle. Four color throughout. 80p. $24.95.

Hills, Henry. **Making Money**. 72p. $7.50. VHS videotape $24.95.
  Book & tape $29.95.

Huang Yunte. **SHI: A Radical Reading of Chinese Poetry**. 76p. $9.95

Hunt, Erica. **Local History**. 80 p. $9.95.

Kuszai, Joel (editor) **poetics@**, 192 p. $13.95.

Inman, P. **Criss Cross**. 64 p. $7.95.

Inman, P. **Red Shift**. 64p. $6.

Lazer, Hank. **Doublespace**. 192 p. $12.

Levy, Andrew. **Paper Head Last Lyrics**. 112 p. $11.95.

Mac Low, Jackson. **Representative Works: 1938–1985**. 360p. $18.95 (cloth).

Mac Low, Jackson. **Twenties**. 112p. $8.95.

McMorris, Mark. **The Café at Light**. 112p. $12.95.

Moriarty, Laura. **Rondeaux**. 107p. $8.

Neilson, Melanie. **Civil Noir**. 96p. $8.95.
Osman, Jena. **An Essay in Asterisks**. 112p. $12.95.
Pearson, Ted. **Planetary Gear**. 72p. $8.95.
Perelman, Bob. **Virtual Reality**. 80p. $9.95.
Perelman, Bob. **The Future of Memory**. 120p. $14.95.
Piombino, Nick, **The Boundary of Blur**. 128p. $13.95.
Prize Budget for Boys, **The Spectacular Vernacular Revuew**. 96p. $14.95.
Raworth, Tom. **Clean & Will-Lit**. 106p. $10.95.
Robinson, Kit. **Balance Sheet**. 112p. $11.95.
Robinson, Kit. **Democracy Boulevard**. 104p. $9.95.
Robinson, Kit. **Ice Cubes**. 96p. $6.
Rosenfield, Kim. **Good Morning—MIDNIGHT—**. 112p. $10.95.
Scalapino, Leslie. **Objects in the Terrifying Tense
    Longing from Taking Place**. 88p. $9.95.
Seaton, Peter. **The Son Master**. 64p. $5.
Sherry, James. **Popular Fiction**. 84p. $6.
Silliman, Ron. **The New Sentence**. 200p. $10.
Silliman, Ron. **N/O**. 112p. $10.95.
Smith, Rod. **Music or Honesty**. 96p. $12.95
Smith, Rod. **Protective Immediacy**. 96p. $9.95
Stefans, Brian Kim. **Free Space Comix**. 96p. $9.95
Tarkos, Christophe. **Ma Langue est Poétique—Selected Works**. 96p. $12.95.
Templeton, Fiona. **Cells of Release**. 128p. with photographs. $13.95.
Templeton, Fiona. **YOU—The City**. 150p. $11.95.
Torres, Edwin. **The All-Union Day of the Shock Worker**. 112 p. $10.95.
Tysh, Chris. **Cleavage**. 96p. $11.95.
Ward, Diane. **Human Ceiling**. 80p. $8.95.
Ward, Diane. **Relation**. 64p. $7.50.
Watson, Craig. **Free Will**. 80p. $9.95.
Watten, Barrett. **Progress**. 122p. $7.50.
Weiner, Hannah. **We Speak Silent**. 76 p. $9.95
Weiner, Hannah. **Page**. 136 p. $12.95
Wellman, Mac. **Miniature**. 112 p. $12.95
Wellman, Mac. **Strange Elegies**. 96 p. $12.95
Wolsak, Lissa. **Pen Chants**. 80p. $9.95.
Yasusada, Araki. **Doubled Flowering:
    From the Notebooks of Araki Yasusada**. 272p. $14.95.

ROOF BOOKS are published by
Segue Foundation • 300 Bowery •New York, NY 10012
Visit our website at **segue.org**

ROOF BOOKS are distributed by
SMALL PRESS DISTRIBUTION
1341 Seventh Avenue • Berkeley, CA. 94710-1403.
Phone orders: 800-869-7553
spdbooks.org